Star Light Star Bright
Where the Heck is Mr. Right

A JOURNEY OF
GOOD DATES & GOOD STORIES

Written by
DENISE LIZETTE

Love & Laughter!
Denise Lizette ♡

Illustrated by
JAMIE RUTHENBERG

ISBN: 978-0-578-71811-8

Dedication

To you, the strong, real love-seeking people who are brave enough to keep putting yourselves out there, are self-loving enough to forgive yourself often, know when to walk away, and are smart enough to find the funny in all of life's Good Stories!

May your dating journey be filled with laughter, learning, and great experiences!

"Sometimes the bad things that happen in our lives put us directly on the path to the best things that will ever happen to us.

~ Denise Lizette

CONTENTS

INTRODUCTION

Have you ever been single and dating, and dating, and dating? We have all had at least one phase in our lives when we are single and dating, in some way, shape, or form, right? I, on the other hand, have spent most of my life single and dating.

When I was a very young girl, I had a diary … with a little lock on it, of course. After all, privacy is important! I wrote about childish things, worries, family, friends, boy crushes, social situations and insecurities, dreams, as well as life's beginnings and endings. My diaries turned into journals advancing with age, wisdom, and growth. I still keep a journal. You see, all my life, my diary has given me a space to speak freely, to think clearly, and to vent what needs to be vented without consequence. Honestly, that is how this book began.

I started dating around the age of 18 … late bloomer for sure. After each first date, I would come home and journal my raw thoughts, feelings, first impressions, observations, emotions, overall experiences, places we went, etc. As I started off as just a young woman, navigating my thoughts, feelings, and emotions after every first date, I realized that I was learning a lot about myself. The good, the funny, the bad, the amazing, it all just poured out of me and onto the pages. Sometimes I found myself shaking my head with giggles, other times shaking my head with disgust, and sometimes just smiling with utter delight!

As my dating life started blossoming, I decided to make a separate journal for these reflection moments, and even started numbering the first dates to count how many lifetime first dates I would have. At first, that seemed kind of fun, simple, and comfortable, maybe even unnecessary. *Surely, I would find my husband and stop all this dating in no time!* I thought. Now, 30-plus years later, that "counting thing" surely takes on a whole new meaning. As I embarked on writing this book, my last first date of 2019 was first date #236.

Much has been learned on these dates over the years, logistically, personally, emotionally, and introspectively. I'd say the common thread for me has been learning about human behavior, mine, their's—everyone's!

People fascinate me, always have, always will! What makes us tick, tock, or scream all have deeper definitions. Furthermore, dating for the last 30 years is a life lesson in itself; the process has significantly changed! Who knew that "online anything" was going to replace the good old happenstance meetings I relied on when I was 18? I didn't even have a cell phone at 18 years old! At that point, I would have never thought so many of us would be single in our 40's and beyond, nor would I have thought we would be meeting people through something called the internet!

Over the last 30-plus years, my dating mantra and attitude has always been, "It's a 'Good Date,' or it's a 'Good Story.' Either way, it's all good!" Of course, the "Good Dates" are the first dates I would have hoped for a second or third date. The "Good Stories" are the first dates that were most likely going nowhere fast!

You will find this book is filled with many Good Stories and filtered throughout the Good Stories are my Good Dates. Then there are the men that I consider The Good Ones, who are men that at some point in my life meant a lot to me. In highlighting my most memorable first date experiences, I have placed these dates in categories instead of sequential order. You will see a number associated with each story, which will give you a sense of where they fell in my overall timeline. I have also thrown in what I call "Speed Rounds." The Speed Rounds contain men worth mentioning yet not categorized. These dates will be described in a quick sentence or two, with a sometimes sassy reflection.

My intension in sharing these stories is not only to entertain you, but to also connect with you. Sharing the human experience—at least in the world of single people who are dating to find meaningful love—allows us to feel that we are not alone. We are all in this together! Because of that, I wanted to create a reading experience that has good energy, insight, lots of laughter, and a spice of sarcasm. After all, life is hilarious, if you don't take yourself too seriously!

Chapter One
THE BLIND DATES

#75
Margarita Guy

I met his mother at a golf outing, riding in a golf cart for 18 holes. She shared she had a "really nice son" and I was a "really nice young woman" and that we should definitely meet. Then she asked if I would be interested in going out with her son? Of course, I said yes, and after a quick chat on the phone with him, we decided to go to a Tiger's baseball game together. The plan was for us to meet at a restaurant in Royal Oak for a drink and then we would drive together to the game downtown. So far so good!

When we met, it was clear that he was very nervous, which I took as a compliment.

After our hellos, he said, "I should order you a margarita."

"Actually, I don't drink margarita's," I kindly said to him, "but I would love a vodka and cranberry."

So we got our drinks and chitchatted, and then we left for the game. As we were driving down to the game, he shared that he didn't have tickets. "We'll get them when we get down there," he said, adding that he had a dentist friend who had great seats and should be at the game, too. Apparently, it didn't matter what kind of seats we bought because we would find his friend and sit with him. Okay, great!

We got to the ball park and it was one of those busy times when there were four events going on at once and absolutely no parking anywhere. He decided to parallel park in a spot right next to a sign that said "no parking at any time." I thought, *God only knows if his car will be here at the end of the night!*

Now we just needed tickets. When I asked him where we go to purchase tickets, he answered, "Oh, we will scalp them." I thought, *So far we parked in an illegal spot and we are going to buy our tickets illegally!*

Suddenly, without any explanation, he left me on the sidewalk and ducked into a back alley. Apparently, someone had motioned to him and he knew the signs. A minute later, he came walking out of the alley with two tickets, ready to go.

"Okay, this is great!" he said. "We can go in, go to my favorite little place, and then we can get you a margarita."

After we got into the stadium, we went to the little place with the slushy drinks, and I was now feeling pressured to get some kind of frozen margarita type drink. *What is with this guy and the margarita pressure?* So I partially caved in and got some kind of pink slushy thing, we grabbed a couple of hot dogs, and we finally made it to our seats.

At this point, he started talking about all of his very personal woes in his lifetime. He explained how he had a rough childhood, how he tried to commit suicide twice, and the psychological issues he had been battling. Now I was getting concerned and we weren't even into the third inning!

Then, he began to obsessively hunt down his friend, the dentist. He was calling him, texting him, looking around the park for him, all with no luck. I suggested that we just go back to our seats and relax a bit.

"Okay, before we go back to our seats, do you want me to get you a margarita?" he asked.

"No, I'm good right now. Let's just go back to our seats."

He finally got ahold of his friend and found out what section he was in. As we left our seats, he again said, "We should go get you a margarita."

"No, I'm fine with what I have. ..." *What is happening right now?*

We finally found his dentist friend and his wife, who appeared to be perfectly normal and very friendly people. My date also appeared to be more comfortable now that we were with them and was very chatty, at one point explaining what had happened so far on our date—almost like he was checking with them to see how they thought it was going.

The game finally ended and he suggested that we all go to a well-known local bar. I immediately thought, *I think we should go check to see if the car is still there!* However, we went straight to the bar to grab some appetizers, and yes, as we were ordering, he again asked if he should order me a margarita.

His friend interrupted, "Dude, seriously! She does not want a margarita! I don't know why you keep asking her this! She has said 'no' four times!"

"Thank you for asking, but I am okay right now," I concluded with a gracious smile.

Thankfully, the night ended shortly after and we walked back to the car—or at least I was hoping we were going to find his car still there. We turned the corner and low and behold the car was there! *Thank God!*

So I got into his car, ignoring the fact that he was coming around to chivalrously get my door for me. I thought, *Forget that! Let's just go!* He then got in the car as well, but now he could not find his keys. He searched and searched, and finally found the keys on the dashboard! Yes, I said the dashboard ... and right in the heart of downtown Detroit! The fact that this car was still there waiting for us was a miracle!

We finally pulled up to my parked car behind the restaurant where this all started. It was a full day and all I wanted to do was fly out of his car, get in mine, and drive home.

At the time, I drove a Grand Prix with a small spoiler on the back. That said, what did I see as we finally drove up to my car? Six large cans of beer lined up across the spoiler of my car! At this point, nothing was surprising anymore!

I got out of the car, cleared the beer cans, waved goodbye to him as he drove away, and then sat alone in silence for five seconds. I suddenly burst out laughing. I think I laughed for at least 10 minutes of my ride home. *What was all that?*

There is no such thing as an "ugly baby," ... especially if it is a mother's son.

#69
My Wax Lady's Son

Within the first ten minutes of lunch, I knew the number of guns he owned, the number of cigarettes he smoked a day, and how many times a week he got high. Luckily, that was a short date that afterword I made sure not to discuss with his mother.

Good intention by my wax lady, but too many deal breakers for me!

#53
A Holiday Party with a Corsage!

In my mid-twenties, I worked at the corporate offices of a national, new home construction company and had friends that worked at the same company's regional office. The regional office always had legendary Christmas parties so my friends, Will and Allison (mostly Allison), wanted me to come to this particular year's Christmas event. It was going to be held at the Renaissance Center in downtown Detroit, with a casino night theme. So they conjured up a date for me to gain access and we had a blind double date to the Christmas party. When my date was described to me, he sounded cute, nice, was from Michigan's upper peninsula, and worked as a project manager. Perfect! The important part was that we were going to the party!

That night, I was at Will and Allison's house having cocktails while waiting for my date. When he showed up, he was holding something very interesting that I couldn't make out at first. I thought, *Is that a bowl of water with flowers in it? Did he bring me a flower? That was very kind.*

Well, it was a flower alright—a big corsage was floating in a glass bowl of water. What was I supposed to do with this? Pin a wet corsage to my brand new dress?

Allison was trying not to bust out laughing as she took me aside. "Denise, you cannot wear that corsage to this party. You just can't!"

"I know, right?" I said, also doing all I could not to laugh too loudly.

"This is what we are going to do. We are going to rush! We're just going to rush out the door and then say, 'Oops, we forgot it. No big deal,' and move on with night."

Sticking to our genius plan, we were both frantically hustling to get on our coats and get out the door. My date was the first person to walk out, followed by the rest of us. Suddenly, he turned around.

"Oh, wait! We forgot Denise's corsage," he said.

Feeling defeated, we went back in and pinned the infamous wet corsage to my dress and left.

During the car ride down, I knew I could not walk into this party looking like a tenth grade homecoming date. As sweet as this seemed, I just could not do it. Then, it came to me.

"This is such a lovely corsage. I really do think I should leave it safely in the car so that it doesn't get smashed. I am going to be hugging people—it's definitely going to get smashed, and I won't be able to look at it tomorrow."

Allison kept looking forward in the front seat, but I saw her shoulders subtly shake as she quietly died laughing. Thankfully, he seemed okay with this idea and I quickly removed the corsage. *Thank God!*

But the story doesn't end there.

Once we got to the party, I pretty much hit the ground running and had a great time talking to people I hadn't seen in quite a while. To be honest, I paid no attention to what he was doing for the entire evening. Whether that was good or bad on my part, it was what it was. Apparently, he stood by Will for part of the night, asking Will if he thought I was into him.

On the way home, my date and I were again in the back seat. As we started for home, he began to inch over. Then more and more, to the point where my face was literally against the window glass so to not be touched by this man. Remember that cartoon character, Garfield? That car version with the suction cup paws that people used to stick inside their car windows? If you do remember, that was totally me!

He wasn't trying to hold my hand. He clearly was trying to make out! My friends were in the front seat of the car! What was he thinking? At this point, I was convinced that he was out of his mind. I asked him to please stop, which actually shocked him.

When we reached Will and Allison's home, Will asked if either of us needed to come in, if we were okay to drive, etc. Both of us said we were fine. As I said, I spent the night paying zero attention to what my date was doing. As we walked to my car, I realized that he obviously was extremely drunk, to the point where Will wanted him to stay at their house instead of driving.

"No I'm just fine. No worries," he said as he staggered over to his car. I slithered into my car as fast as I could, put the key into the ignition, and situated myself for the drive. When I looked up to pull out, he was standing, peeing on their front lawn, right by his car! Right in front of me … in front of everyone! Apparently, he decided that he had to go after all. We were in an affluent neighborhood. What was he thinking? I watched the steady stream hitting their lawn, and I laughed with a sigh of gratitude as I pulled away from their house.

Nothing was funnier than the next day when Allison called me.

"Denise, did you see what happened at the end? Hysterical!" she laughed.

To this day, Allison and I can't help but laugh at the unforgettable "night of the corsage." Truthfully, his intentions were extremely sincere, but as it is often said, timing is everything, and in all fairness ... I wasn't a very good date either!

CAUTION: Be careful what you wish for when you ask a friend to find you a date!

Chapter Two

WHAT THE WHAT?

#126

The Kick-Ass Date!

We met through a dating service. I joined a legit dating service in my late 30's. They interviewed all their members, matched us and even set reservations for us to meet at a local restaurant. "My match," as they would call it, worked at one of the big three in the automotive industry as a clay sculptor. He actually created models of the new car designs out of clay. Sounds interesting, right?

I arrived a bit early and watched him walk in. He was a very slim man, possibly shorter than me—I am 5'3—and had a darker, ethnic look. He sat down, we chatted for a few minutes, and he seemed very nice. He also seemed very excitable in conversation, which I liked because I am also a very excitable, passionate person.

The server came to take our drink orders. I ordered a glass of red wine, and he ordered the same exact glass of wine. After a few minutes, I ordered my entrée, and again, he ordered the same entrée. Even when I got a refill on my wine, he did the same. I didn't understand why he was following every move I made, but then I thought to just let it go.

We then talked more about the fact that he was no longer working at the automotive company and was now at an art college, recalibrating his career. When hearing this, I thought, *That is EXACTLY where this man needs to be. Fits him perfectly!* His creative vibe was pretty strong. He then mentioned that I reminded him of one of the executives he knew at his previous job named Mandy Roberts. When he said her name, I was shocked! Mandy Roberts lived behind me when I was a little girl and was my babysitter growing up. She has been an executive in the automotive world for years; I was delighted that he knew her, and over the moon that he compared me to her. To this day she is my idol. From the time I was 8 to now almost 50, I have often said, "I want to be just like Mandy when I grow up!"

I felt like I was talking to a much younger person throughout the entire date. He was all over the map in topics, talking about the fact that he was building a fire pit in his backyard ... well, actually his parents' backyard because he lived with them now. I thought, *Okay, no judgment. The downturn of the economy was hard.* However, it got worse as the conversation got more and more "teen-like."

At one point, he said, "I don't know, but this has been a super great date! I can't explain it any other way except 'kick ass!'"

First off, I hadn't heard that phrase in at least 15 years, so I was dying of laughter inside—really couldn't have had to hold back the laughter harder! The kicker is he then stuck his hand up over the booth table waiting for a high five, because this was a "kick ass" date! *What do you do when someone puts his hand up for a high five? You can't leave him hanging there, right?* Feeling compelled to, I high fived him back, surprising myself! Again, inside I was SO giggling.

As we continued talking, we ordered dessert. Of course, he ordered the same exact dessert I did, but he was let down that I didn't order coffee because he really loved coffee with dessert.

"I don't drink coffee, but please order coffee," I insisted.

"Not even an espresso or cappuccino?" he begged.

"No, but please order it for yourself if you want that," I again insisted.

The fact that he wouldn't order anything I wasn't going to order was clear at this moment, so I ordered the coffee, if nothing else for the sake that he finally had something he wanted to order and not just going along with what I wanted! He was a really sweet person.

He then continued talking while we ate our desserts.

"I don't know if you've noticed that people—especially at school—have been doing different stuff with their hair," he said. "Did you notice my hair?"

I was thinking, *I have no idea what I am supposed to be noticing. It's dark in this restaurant and you have dark hair.*

"I'm not really sure what you mean. I guess I didn't," I responded, confused.

"Let me get into the light more, and you can see that I put some blue in my hair! Everyone at school is doing this right now," he said, very excited about this whole idea of blue hair.

"Blue?"

"Yeah! I mean, everybody at the art school is doing different things with their hair. Some are putting pink stripes in it—everyone is doing something, so I had to do something, too! So I decided to put some blue in it! What do you think?"

What do I think? Oh boy ... I just high-fived someone across the table who has blue hair! That's what I think! I think I am glad it is dark in the restaurant and frankly think this date has taken one too many turns for me! What is happening?

Thankfully, we finished dessert and he again said that this was a "kick-ass" date, very excited to possibly go out again. I have to say, he was persistent after that night; he called often, and quickly invited me to a bonfire to meet his parents. Looking back, he was truly a very sweet person. However, timing is everything in terms of where you are in your life. As sweet as he was, he needed someone who was equally sweet ... and naïve. He also needed someone who was as open in creative expression as he was. I wasn't going to be that girl. He may not have seen that fact, but I sure did.

A "kick-ass, high five, and look at my blue hair" kind of date. ... Life is hilarious, even when it doesn't work out!

#98

The Gentle Giant Who Dropped Like a Rock!

So I have what I call "boating friends." These are friends that you see during boating season in Michigan. It is often acknowledged that boating friends have no last name and you rarely know what they do for a living; it's kind of unnecessary! You simply meet these people, in a bathing suit, drink in-hand, and have continuous fun-filled weekends from June to August! My sister and her husband have had boats for years, so the tag-along sister has had the luxury of this fun time for decades.

Over the years, I had many crushes within this group. However, I don't think I really had more than one or two dates with any of these people. In hindsight, these were not my forever type of people. I just kept hoping they would grow to be. ... Anyway, date #98 seemed nice, kind-hearted, and was typically a bit shy or quiet when I would see him on the water. At some point he shared he had a crush on me with his friends and eventually we all went out, met, chatted, etc., which led to him asking for an official date with me.

"A group is going to my cousin's restaurant (also a boating friend) for a friends birthday dinner, then after dinner we are planning to go upstairs to the bar and celebrate more. There is dancing there too. It will be fun!" he shared. All sounded like fun to me.

We arrived at the restaurant; their whole boating crew was together for dinner. He was sitting across from me and I quickly noticed he was drinking three drinks to my one. He was a big guy—probably 6'4" and 300 pounds—but this was a lot of drinking. ... Then again, he's a boater. They are professionals!

One of his buddies said, "Hey man, pace it out," so I was thinking perhaps it was nerves. Either way. ...

We moved on from dinner to the upstairs bar and there was a band playing, so people were dancing. I was out dancing for a little while with some of the girls, and then I walked over to him, who was sitting at the bar with his buddies. As I was approaching, he stood up, took one step forward toward the dance floor, as to let me into the space he was sitting, and then he literally dropped. This 6'4" guy took a dead weight fall right onto the little dance floor. BOOM! He was down fast and loud. I was in total shock. His cousins and friends went to him quickly and were trying to wake him up. He was out cold! It may have been 45-60 seconds. It felt like forever, but he woke up and then stood right up!

"Are you okay, buddy? What happened?" his friends were asking as they helped him up.

"I'm fine. Totally fine. Where is Denise?" he said. His buddies were a little confused. Then, as he saw me, he began to walk over to me.

"What just happened?" I anxiously asked him. "Please don't ever do that again—you scared me half to death! What just happened?"

He looked confused. "What do you mean what just happened?"

"No seriously, what just happened? You just stood up and then fell!"

"No I didn't."

"Yes you did! Everybody here saw you." *He has no recollection of this happening!*

A woman who was standing next to me said, "You just completely fell! You are totally freaking her out. What just happened?"

"I don't know. We're okay," he said. "I was just going to run to the bathroom. I will be right back. I have no idea what you guys are talking about."

I realized that he really had no recollection of this and I was still reeling from my own panic, so as he went to the bathroom I took a breath and tried to calm down.

Shortly after, we decided it was time to leave. I insisted on driving, offering my couch for him to crash for the night.

"Oh no no, I am totally fine," he strongly insisted. "I am driving you home."

"No you are not. I am driving. You just fell down!"

"I don't know why you keep saying that—I didn't. Get in the car. I am driving."

To be honest with you, I don't know why I conformed to this decision in the end. I felt he was becoming a little unstable, literally and figuratively I guess, and I had a moment of thinking, *Don't rock the boat.* On the way home, there was no conversation in the car other than my conversation with God, which was perfect because at that moment of "What the what?" and "Please get us home safely," any conversation with him would have fallen on deaf ears.

When we got to my house, I once again insisted he stay on the couch but he refused. "No, I'm good. I think I know where I am." *I think I know where I am?* At this point, there was nothing I could do to stop him from driving home.

The next day, he called me.

"Oh my gosh, you are not going to believe this. I talked to three or four people that were at the bar last night and they all said I fell. Are they just messing with me? What the hell!"

I told you the same thing at least nine times last night, and now you are calling me for validation? Seriously how did you even find your way home?...Oh boy!

"Yes, you fell, and you scared the hell out of me. It wasn't pretty," I answered. "Then you drove me home, and then yourself home, which I don't even know how you did. It was scary."

"I don't believe this. Well, next time, I promise that won't happen."

Honey, I am sorry but there will not be a next time.

As over-the-top crazy as this whole thing was, there was something just as over the top naïve or childlike about him. I still see him once or twice a year, either at a grocery store or on the water. He is still a crazy drinker—now utilizing ride sharing services, thank God—and I think he still doesn't remember what happened that night. He consistently tries to ask me out again and again, almost every time I see him. He means no harm, no malice or creepy intentions and never did—he just scared the hell out of me!

Just a simple and kindhearted guy, with an unforeseen bang to the story!

Chapter Three

ONE OF THE GOOD ONES:

#8
My First Everything

Around 20 years old, I met #8 at a housewarming party for two of the girls I worked with at a shoe store. I vividly remember I was sitting on their couch and saw a cute guy peek his head out from the kitchen, look right at me, and then disappear back into the kitchen. He then did it once more, and then asked one of girls, "Who is the redhead on the couch?" That was the night it all started.

Honestly, I do not remember details of a first date because we did not start with that kind of a structured relationship. We first met at this particular party and then we would continuously see each other out at the bar, which lead to intentional meet-ups at the bar, which then lead to an exclusive relationship.

He was attractive, fun, liked to dance, a little older than me, was in the service and now the reserves. He had all the checks to my boxes, at that moment in time. This was my first "serious" relationship, which lead to my first everything. My first boyfriend. My first love. The first man I was intimate with. The first family that I embraced as my own and enjoyed every bit of the experience.

Of course, this didn't last a lifetime. How could it? I was young, learning, trying, pushing for changes in our relationship that were not going to happen, all as he was showing me a selfishness that wasn't kind. He had insecurities that he didn't know how to process without putting me down, to make himself feel better. On many levels this man was so many lessons all wrapped in one.

I had lost my father about 6 months before I met him. That definitely played a part in me diving in and attaching so many feelings to this relation-ship. At first, as a young woman, I wanted attention from a man, a boyfriend etc. Then, after I got that attention, I realized it wasn't just the attention I needed; I needed qualities, values, respect, and a different definition of love that he was not willing (or maybe capable) to give.

We broke up after about 2 years. I had a hard time not keeping in touch with his mom, who I really liked. Isn't that what just happens some-times? I learned so much and will always appreciate my first everything!

Things worked out as they should. They always do!

Chapter Four
THE ENGINEERS

ENGINEERS

en·gi·neer | \enjuh-nir\
noun

Professionals who invent, design, analyze, build and test machines, complex systems, structures, and materials to fulfill functional objectives and requirements while considering the limitations imposed by practicality, regulation, safety, and cost.

#160
The Super Bowl Snowstorm

It was Super Bowl Sunday and a Michigan blizzard was forecasted. We decided on a casual date at his house to eat, drink and watch the big game. Sounds fun. I'm in!

As I got ready, he texted me suggesting that I leave for his house a little earlier because of the snow that was already coming down, so I did just that. Off I went into the snowstorm and what was supposed to be about a 35-minute drive became an hour-plus, as snow kept falling.

As I got closer, I got a text saying that he is sorry that he didn't shovel; he took a shower and he didn't want to get sweaty. ... *What?*

I went to pull into the drive, then quickly stopped and parked at the end of the driveway, thinking, *There is a lot of snow. I may not make it up the drive in my car.* I walked through the piling snow, up the pathway, and up to the porch. As he opened the door, I glanced over to see that he had shoveled a one-shovel width path around his car. ... Hmm. ...

"Oh, hi. How are you?" he said with a warm smile, in a very sweet, oblivious manner.

"Wow, it looks like it's really coming down out here, huh?" he said.

"Yeah, it is."

I was a little stressed from driving in the snow, so it took a moment, but after coming into the house and unloading my things, I took a deep breath and was ready to get going on the super bowl food and festivities. I had brought a dip that I make and I asked him to try it. He wouldn't try mine until after I tried his first, so I did, and it was good. It was avocado based, also, and surprisingly similar to mine—kind of ironic. After he took a taste of my dip, he stood there a moment.

"Well, ya know, I think it's okay. ..." I then watched as he continued to scoff the entire thing down.

I looked over at the television and saw that the Super Bowl pre-game show was coming on soon. To be honest, I don't usually watch professional football, but I do love watching the Super Bowl. I like watching the pregame hype; I like to see what the President is going to predict. For some reason, I enjoy this stuff–there is something about the WOW of it all that is exciting to me.

So, as we gathered our drinks and snacks and settled in the family room, he turned to me and said, "Let's watch a movie." *What? A movie?* He then proceeded to pick out a pre-civil war western. *What is happening? Why would we start a movie when we are 40 minutes to kickoff?* The movie started playing and as we approached the pre-game hype, I suggested we stop the movie and watch the pre game "stuff." He wasn't certain that it was a good place to stop the movie. So, fifteen minutes later, we stopped the movie—at a "good place."

Ultimately, we did get to see about 15 minutes of pregame and then proceeded to watch the game. As we were watching, my attention shifted, less on the game and more on what was happening outside the huge picture window that spanned across the back of his family room. All I could see was the snow that was getting heavier and heavier, and the path around his car that he so carefully shoveled was no longer there. The snow was piling higher on top of his car and windshield (with the windshield wipers pulled outward so not to stick to the windshield, a total engineer move!).

Once the game was over and we finished the movie, it was close to midnight and the snow was slowing down but was also ridiculously high.

He turned to me and said, "Well, ya know, I would ask you to stay and crash on the couch because of the snow, but I have to get up early tomorrow morning, so …"

So … what? Have you lost your mind? I drive a small vehicle—there is nine feet of snow out there!

Then he continued with, "Tell you what, I will go brush off your car and shovel a path to your car for you."

Now, I was convinced that after seeing that we literally had 16 inches of snow on the ground while shoveling he would think twice about me driving, and say, "It really is bad out there. Even though I have to get up really early, I think it is safer if you stay here."

I gathered my things, pulled on my boots, and bundled up. As he was halfway through shoveling, he reminded me to pre-heat my car.

"It should be warmed up by the time I am done."

He came back in the house, said goodbye, and I walked to the car, where I heard young boys yelling, "Hey lady, do you need help? Are you driving in this?"

"Yes, I am going to try," I replied.

"We'll watch and come help if you get stuck!" they yelled back.
So there I was sitting in the car, staring out the wet windshield for a moment. The nose of my car was facing the front door, which was already shut. No one was standing in the window; lights were out. Those young boys had more chivalry in he last two minutes than he had all night. I took a deep breath. I prayed a moment and told myself *slow and steady.*

I backed my car up a bit and I thought, *It's working.* I got down the street. *It's working.* Then, the next street, and the next. Miraculously, two and a half hours later, I managed to make it home safely. I texted him when I got home. He didn't reply until the next morning.

About mid morning the next day, I finally got a text reply from him saying, "Oh my gosh, the roads were SO bad this morning! Like, REALLY BAD. It took my over an hour to get to work! I can't believe what I just went through! That was terrible." … *Really?*

How is it that something only exists when they experience it? When another person experiences the same thing, not so much! An engineer he was. He focused on his lane, and his lane only.

#223
I'm In Sales. ... Nope. You Are an Engineer!

We met online and, after only a few days of talking, we decided to meet. He was leaving on a family vacation soon and wanted to meet before. All good! He picked the place and I arrived on time.

As I sat down, my phone buzzed with a text. "Just leaving my house." I figured he would be another 15 minutes; life happens! So, what I thought would be a fifteen-minute wait turned into 35 minutes of waiting with my drink, chips, and salsa.

He finally arrived and stood at the end of the booth.

"You're not going to stand up and hug me?" he asked.

I looked up and said, "No I am not."

He then sat down across from me and I noticed he was wearing his sunglasses backwards—one of my pet peeves—and he wore them that way for the entire time we were at dinner. He proceeded to dive right into talking all about himself and his current situation. This included the fact that he was freshly divorced and was diving headfirst into the dating scene, utilizing several dating sites and in that "quantity" mode that some people fall into.

He spoke further about the fact that he was in "automotive sales." I find that the engineers who are in automotive sales (account managers or representatives) think they are in sales. Honestly, this always makes me laugh! Their jobs don't have any heavy lead generation, nor cold calling. They have 10-year corporate contracts of which they project manage the terms and production. Yes there is a buy and/or sell of something in that contract ... and that something is something engineered! UGH!

"I just went on a date with a real estate agent, and she is going to turn fifty next year, just like you," he said to me.

"Oh really. Interesting."

"Yeah, and we actually came here. As a matter of fact, we sat in this same booth," he added.

"Oh … Okay. …"

"So she's going to be turning fifty and she was telling me that she wants to be married by the time she is fifty, and she knows exactly what she wants her ring to look like. So what do you want your ring to look like?"

What? What are we talking about?

"Well, I don't know if I have that identified at this point. I'm looking for a relationship first. I'll figure out the ring thing later—I guess I don't really feel the need to have timelines for these things," I answered.

"Well, she was very adamant, and she also said that she is the top real estate agent in the state—absolute number one in the state. She is super successful."

"That's great."

Being a real estate agent myself, there is no way he was dating the best agent in the state. She was married. I tried to clarify if we were speaking of the same person and he replied.

"No, I don't think that was her name," he answered, adding, "but she is really good. So how much business do you do? Are you even good?"

Why are we having this conversation? This man is offensive and truly clueless!

Then, he went one step further.

"Well, ya know, she's in real estate, she's almost fifty, she is obviously going through her own kind of mid-life crisis, *and* she needs a man. So how bad do *you* need a man?"

At this point, I lost it. In my condescending voice, which no one likes—including me—I responded.

"I am NOT sure why we are having this conversation. I am NOT sure why you continuously are bringing up some woman you dated, which obviously didn't work out. The fact that I have to compare myself to her, and/or maybe you think I have to compete with her, is beyond ridiculous! I really don't care about this woman! I am here to learn about you and I thought you were here to learn about me. If that's what we are going to do—excellent! If not, then I am not sure why we are here!"

He stared at me with the look of *What was that all about?*

"Well, if *YOU* are so good at asking questions and *I* am so terrible at it, then why don't you ask the rest of the questions," he responded, exposing his inner child. I almost burst out laughing!

At that point, I decided instead of asking a question, I would take a beat, sip on my cocktail, and let it be silent for a minute or two. Then, I shared a bit of dating advice and interestingly, he listened. After quickly eating we went on our way.

About 5 months later, around Thanksgiving, he texted me. "Hope you had a fantastic Thanksgiving."

I didn't recognize the number, so I replied in kind and asked who this was.

He responded with his picture and name. "From the summer. See you are back online dating."

I didn't respond.

Next text bubble from him. "Ahha, not interested?"

No response again.

Next text bubble. "Sorry. I completely forgot."

The "know it all" automotive sales person (aka engineer) who forgot it all was clearly still a dating disaster!

Chapter Five
ONE OF THE GOOD ONES:

#10
My Prince On a White Horse

He was a human resources consultant for the company I worked for. Always friendly, nicely built, good-looking, successful, smart, and very charismatic. One day, he needed copies made but there was some confusion as to where I would find what I needed to be copied, so he came with me to help find the documents. While we were working on this, he said he would be wrapped up around 6:00 and asked if I would want to meet him for dinner. I immediately said, "Yes," to my own surprise! At the time, I was dating someone—or should I say I needed to be NOT dating this particular someone, but hadn't broken up with him just yet. In any case, it felt right to say yes, so I did.

I remember coming home before leaving for the restaurant and talking to my mom about this.

"This consultant guy who seems really nice and has been in town for a few weeks asked me out for dinner, and I kinda think it's a date. I mean, I think it might be a date. I am not really sure. ..." I was not yet 21 years old and very naïve.

My mom answered, "I'm sure it's a date."

"You think? He is really nice. He's originally from Ann Arbor, but he lives in Philadelphia right now."

"He's from Ann Arbor?" my mom asked. "What's his last name?"

"Blumberg," I answered.

"Oh, so he's Jewish?"

"I am not sure. Ya think?" I innocently asked. Did I say I was naïve?

My mom smiled. "Yes, I think." Looking back, this conversation cracks me up because of course it was a date, and what part of Blumberg isn't Jewish?

We went to a nice restaurant located in a Rochester Village and had a wonderful dinner. When we were done, we walked around the mall together, and then sat on his car and talked and talked and talked. We had a fantastic time.

The next day, he left for Philadelphia and began to call me often. Recognizing this could very well be my prince on a white horse, I could not let him pass me by, so I broke up with the old guy (#8) and didn't look back.

For our second date, he invited me to go with him to a wedding ... in Colorado! He was going to fly me out there, meet his good friends, golf, have a great time, and enjoy the beautiful wedding!

He met me at the airport, picked me up, and drove me straight to the golf course, where all of the guys in the wedding party were together for a bachelor-type round of golf. Being not the best golfer at the time, and the only female on the whole course, we separated from the guys, which was very sweet of him. We thoroughly enjoyed Colorado and had an INCREDIBLE time.

After the Colorado trip in August, he was coming back to Michigan often. Being from Ann Arbor, he was a huge University of Michigan fan. We would go to games, celebrate a few holidays, see each other often, and I was completely enamored with him.

It was around the holidays, and for the first time I was going to fly out to Philadelphia to stay with him and see where he lived. While I was there, we went shopping for holiday gifts and went into to the historic department store called Wanamakers (it was most famous for being featured in the movie *The Mannequin*) where he bought me the most adorable holiday stuffed animal, named Twinkles. Twinkles was a reindeer or moose with bells on his ears. We bought many things that day, and I remember him saying Twinkles was his favorite purchase of the day, because the way I lit up when I saw Twinkles in the store; it was innocent and beautiful.

He drove me to the airport after the weekend concluded, luggage checked and Twinkles in hand. I was an over packer and Twinkles was not going to fit in the luggage, and I certainly wasn't leaving him! He walked me to the gate (because back then you could) and as we waited for the plane to start boarding ... he broke up with me. Right there.

Needless to say, I was beyond heartbroken. Looking back, I can't help but laugh at what happened next on the plane ride home. I held it together in front of him and then the devastation, sadness, and out of control crying overtook me as I found my seat on the plane. I couldn't stop crying, all while squeezing Twinkles like an infant child. The poor passengers around me had. to watch this young woman sob, listening to the annoying waves of jingling bells on Twinkles ears for the entire two hour flight! No one said a thing, which tells me I was such a wreck that no one knew what to do with me.

Although my heart was broken, in the end, his elegance, chivalrous manners and beautiful energy will always be cherished. As for Twinkles, I still bring him out every holiday season with a heartwarming smile and glance back to a wonderful memory, a wonderful time, a wonderful guy, and yes, one of the good ones.

This man was definitely my fairy tale prince on a white horse. One of those people that swooped into your life to highlight, excite, and remind you of what love should look, feel, and be like. It wasn't meant to be for us. However, it was a beautiful wake up call that I desperately needed.

Your prince will come. He may not be on a white horse or live in a big castle, but he will want you, and only you, and that will be better than any fairytale

Chapter Six

SPEED ROUND: B.C.
(BEFORE COMMITMENT)

#2 First time I ever saw a "one hitter" joint. He got high (that is not my thing, then or now) and then yelled out the window for miles!

#7 Blind date. I knew we were going nowhere when he stated that he couldn't believe his handicapped sister actually found someone to love and marry her! WOW! Where is the compassion, man?

#14 He looked like a Dr. Seuss character. I couldn't take him seriously.

#16 The date started out as a joke—he needed a "Rent a Wife" for a wedding. Turned into a date with a "grope-ie" man with chronic halitosis! Oh boy!

#22 Engineer. I yawned and he put his finger in my mouth! WHAT?

#26 Drunk guy on St Patrick's Day. Dumb as a box of rocks! He was very surprised I knew where M59 was (major highway in the metro Detroit area)! He must have been dealing with some really dumb women in the past!

#31 Dressed in a sweater and construction boots in the middle of August! WOW! That appeared very HOT in a very unsexy way! And then … did you really not bring a wallet to our date? He fumbled, stammered, and then had no choice but to admit that he didn't have his wallet. An honest mistake, but his ego had a tough time getting those words out! Years later while out with my sister, we saw him at a bar and she confronted him and made him buy us all a round of shots! Hilarious!

#45   This guy didn't stand a chance. I got fired that day. By the time I met up with the friend that was attempting to set me up, I was trashed and absolutely not in the mind frame to meet someone new. Poor guy! I guess I gave him a good story!

#48   Sometimes people surround themselves with fun people, but they themselves are not fun!

#49   Couldn't understand that the phrase "passed away" was a polite way of saying my dad had died when I was 19 years old.

#57 Tennis pro. Arrived in his prime "Miami Vice" ensemble. Blue sport coat, white shirt, and jeans, with a special splash of tennis shoes as his foot-wear—and back then (1999) tennis shoes were NOT worn with any sport coat. Shoes are important people!

#60 & #235   Fixed up with the same guy twice, 20 years in between! Apparently sometimes my memory isn't so good, and neither was his!

#62   Met at a wedding and dated for a little while! WOW! Only way to describe this one is "started good and then went bad like a head of lettuce!" ICK!

#63   The youngest guy I have ever dated. So sweet! We dated for a while. I was his first everything, and then I realized he needed to spread his wings and fly … and fly he did! Always sweet memories and thoughts for this one!

#71   Blind date. His feedback was that I was too Neiman Marcus and he was looking for Eddie Bauer. I'll take that as a compliment.

#73   Nice guy. I tried to pass him forward to someone I thought he would be "perfect" for. … Well, I quickly learned that men don't like that at all!

#76   Let's sum this up in two statements: "dutch treat" and "11/28 birthday." (Ugh! Sagittarians.)

#78   A guy who was on his first, first date in 12 years. Nice guy! Just wanted to get back into life again. Oh, how I can empathize with that!

#106   As old as my mother, rich, and creepy. Blind double date with friends his age. I was the only one who could read the print on the bill without glasses. He really thought highly of himself, and also thought there was going to be a sexual encounter, until he went for the big kiss. His creepy tongue came right at my face and I gave him my cheek! No one should have to encounter this level of creepiness!

#108   Description was, "He is in sales." Reality was he was an engineer. … Need I go on? NEXT!

#114 Who would have thought my little knowledge of the game of cricket could turn a "destine for dooms day" date into a nice dinner conversation. Sometimes you just make it through the date in the best way possible, no harm, no foul.

#122 He gave me the "hope to hear from you" line. Why do men say that? Call me. Women will never tire of a man being a man!

NO DATE BUT NOTABLE I was having a conversation with someone at a restaurant and he darted to his car to brag, prove, and bring in an article written about him in a magazine. What?

NO DATE BUT NOTABLE My sister met this guy at work who she said looked like Keanu Reeves. He got my number, called, and within minutes asked, "So are you hot?" He continued to say, "I dated this 40-something lady and she had two kids but she was hot enough to date." ... OH BOY! Let's polish up that approach! Hence no date!

#131 Stop touching me. He wouldn't stop touching me! Super buggie! And he looked like Richard Simons. OH LORD!

Don't get discouraged by what you are going through. Your time is coming, where you are is not where you are going to stay.

Chapter Seven

ONE OF THE GOOD ONES:

#82

Smitten

It was June of 2002, and I was a project manager at a national health care organization and he was a senior accountant in the corporate accounting department at the same organization. A few of my co-workers kept telling me that I needed to meet this guy in accounting.

"He's really cute, and he is really nice. I think you two would hit it off! You need to meet him!" I would hear this, over and over again.

They kept saying his last name and I kept associating it with another guy in accounting, who was married with kids. I remember thinking, Why do they want me to break up a marriage?

Fast forward to a party I attended for a colleague of ours who just finished his Master's degree. Some of the matchmaker co-workers were at the party.

"Oh, Denise, guess who is here? The guy we really want you to meet. You know, that man we've been talking about. He's here!" one of my co-workers said to me.

"Isn't he married? I went into his office and saw all of these pictures of his family."

"What? No he is not married."
I laughed and explained my confusion with the names. We all laughed, as I realized that the married guy was not #82, thankfully.

As the evening progressed, he came over and chatted with me. He was charming, great smile, eyes, and easy to talk to. I left early, said my goodbyes, and drove home thinking, *Hmmm … he was nice. I'm hopeful!*

The next morning, when I went into the office, I had two voicemail messages on my desktop work phone, both from the matchmaker co-workers.

"Hi Denise, one of my friends—the one that we told you was really going to like you—was talking about you after you left last night. I believe the word that he used was 'smitten.'"

Then there was the next voicemail message.

"Denise, he really likes you! I hope you are looking cute today because I am coming over to get you and we are going to his office upstairs." Minutes later, she was at my door.

We walked together to his office on the next floor of the building, and when we walked in, it was funny to me how incredibly nervous he became. It was as if he was saying to himself, "Oh my God, oh my God, she's in my office!" over and over in his mind. Later in our relationship, there was an inside joke between us on this thought process and experience. We would always laugh that he had two different personas; there was his super-serious-work-self and his fun-after-hours-self—and apparently the two couldn't mix in his world. We did actually talk for a bit that morning, and he seemed to calm down and live through the crossing of the two personas. Ironically, I had just given my notice to my boss because I was going to leave the company and start my real estate career. This worked out well because he could then keep his super-serious-work-self pure, which was hilarious to me!

We began chatting and texting, and he ended up asking me out. I happily said yes! When he came to pick me up, I was living with my mother at the time. My niece and nephew were very little, and my mom's house was filled with high chairs and children's toys. We even had a large playhouse with a slide in the middle of the family room. When he came into the house to pick me up, I did not think twice about the toys, slide, and high chairs—it never even dawned on me to explain because they were like permanent fixtures, just like the furniture in the room.

After the dinner, he drove me back home, gave me a hug good bye, and I walked back into the house. I stood there for a moment and it finally dawned on me! "He must think I have nine kids!" I said to myself. Again, later in the relationship, he said that he just thought that I had kids and they weren't there at the moment. What was more interesting to him was how big my house was—another funny joke between us!

Soon, we had gone out on a couple of dates, but we still had not kissed. We were planning on going out to Birmingham for dinner and drinks together. We ended up at a very crowded bar after dinner, and we were looking for a little pocket of space to stand as the band played. I was just dying to kiss him, so as he was moving to look for a space, I grabbed his hand and pulled him back to me, and kissed him! It was a good kiss and spoken of often. He would always remind me that I kissed him first—he loved it!

We were both quite smitten with one another, and we dated for several months. We then moved into a mode where we were "on again, off again" until we got engaged in 2006, four years after we first met. I ended up breaking this engagement off because I felt he wasn't ready for marriage, or maybe better stated, not in line with my vision of marriage. It was extremely heart wrenching to break the engagement. I loved him very much. Again, we had dated on-and-off for two years after the broken engagement, and then broke up for a full year without contact, which was the longest "off" we had ever had.

He then reached out in 2009 and we caught a drink together to "catch up." That would be forever known as our last "first date." We were engaged within the year, and married shortly after that. Unfortunately, the marriage only lasted two years. However, the memories of our first dates and relationship will always be smiled upon. I loved him very much, so much so that I married him, with high hopes of happiness.

No regrets. I needed to marry him to get behind the curtain and see who he really was, clearly. Unfortunately, who he really was wasn't enough.

Chapter Eight
THE NARCISSISTS

Quick warning: this chapter has a different tone all together. Where I definitely put these in the Good Story category, I'll be honest in saying it is only because I have survived these mountains of pain and disappointment. I also have to openly confess this is where I have struggled, fallen, and experienced a lot of heartache for the majority of my single and dating life. From literally my first boyfriend #8 to my ex-husband, again with the first guy I dated after my divorce, to encounters that just occurred in 2019, I struggle with the narcissistic type of man. They have been very attractive to me (and are to most of us). They are charismatic, they are fun, they appear confident, they appear sincere, typically they are successful, and often times come in with a swoop effect, captivating you before you know it. The narcissist type men are definitely attracted to me because of my open approach, helpful and giving nature, positive disposition, overall looks, and the good heartedness that I have always had. To a narcissist this is a total jackpot! They look good with someone who looks good, which is always key. They have someone they feel they can control, because of my kind nature. They love the supportive nature I have, and use that eventually to raise themselves up while they push another down.

This isn't meant to be a "poor me" moment. I have had those moments for sure. However, where was that going to take me? The only way past these situations is through learning as I go as to how to avoid them—sometimes I learned a lot and other times I learned just a little. Much of this has to do with my thoughts and feelings about myself. My insecurities at certain times in my life played a huge role in how I allowed these men to do what they wanted to do, to get what they wanted to get. When I lost my father at 19, when I got a divorce ... these moments of time where I questioned me and everything in my life, had me open and vulnerable and I kept repeating this pattern on large and small scales!

30-plus years later I think I have a much better grip on this, and 30-plus years later I can laugh at these dates or experiences, along with knowingly shake my head at the narcissistic man that thinks he knows better. 30-plus years later I know who I am and I also know who they are not … not for me!

#170

I met #170 at a sales boot camp put on by the real estate franchise we both worked at. Everyone knew him. At 6'4", he had a grand stature and always commanded a room with his voice and charisma.

He came in on the second week of the ten weeklong class and sat right next to me. Naturally, we started chatting. At first, I couldn't tell whether he was flirting with me or not. My first gut feeling was that I wasn't sure about him; I was sensing something but I couldn't place what it was.

About the third week into the class, he asked me out to dinner. I was enjoying the attention, and ultimately thought it was very sweet how he asked because he let me know how very nervous he was to do so. The night of our date, it was a warm, early September evening and we sat out on the patio of a local restaurant, enjoying drinks and dinner. After, we went walking through downtown Rochester together and sat outside at another beautiful local bar for a drink. He was very charming and we were truly having a wonderful time. At one point, I left to use the restroom and he actually asked everyone around us if they thought he had a chance with me because he wasn't sure. The crowd all agreed that I was "totally into him," and they were right. We then left and walked to a billiards place right on Main Street. Again, in his own charming way, he stopped for a brief moment on our way there and kissed me in the middle of the sidewalk.

Needless to say, after that night it became a whirlwind romance. We saw each other everyday for 30 days straight. We actually counted them out! I met his family; he met mine. He invited me to go on a trip to Mexico to celebrate his mother's birthday, and it was great! There was so much synergy between us. The whole thing seemed to be very "simpatico" on many different levels.

Now we were a couple months into the relationship and facing the holiday season. That was when his insecurities started to come to the surface and things started to get interesting. Word was starting to get out amongst the brokerage locations that we were dating. Some people were saying, "Wow, you are dating Denise? She's amazing!" or "How did you pull that off?" Instead of being flattered or allowing the comments to stroke his ego, he thought, "They like you more," and was offended. One time he literally asked me, "Why do these people like you." I remember looking at him thinking, *What the hell is wrong with you?* I believe I answered, "Maybe because I am a good person. Almost all of these people know me because I helped them with their business." *Why am I defending myself? This is absurd!* He knew why people liked me; it's why he liked me, but he was in such competition with me and at that time he couldn't see past the "they like you more" mindset.

The situation escalated with the "after holiday" parties that my brokerage threw in January. He didn't see why he should have to attend … blah blah! This man hated the fact that people wanted to talk to me, and that they liked and respected me. He hated the attention I received—he should have been the only one getting all of the attention. At that point, he started stepping away from the relationship to try to manipulate, gain control or, even better, have me chase after him. As a result, the relationship shifted toward a void of any affection, physically or emotionally, which is a classic tactic of a narcissist. As I always say, they do what they need to do to get what they want to get. Then, after they show their true colors, they expect you to still be enamored with them and stay with them after they stop doing what you were attracted to in the first place.

I met this man a few years after my divorce and he was the first serious, exclusive relationship that I had after my divorce … and here it was again, my pattern of believing the lying narcissistic man. My ex-husband was also a classic narcissist, and the more I saw the same characteristics, the more I had to admit to myself that I allowed this to happen. I was angry with myself because I got involved with this toxic personality type once again! This was also a tough realization because now I had to detach from him, which has never been an easy thing for me to do in intimate relationships.

A few days after I broke things off, he stopped by to get his stuff from my house and to plead his case on why we should stay together.

"You mean you would rather be alone? Having a relationship when we just see each other once a week isn't better than being alone?"

What was that? I should settle for the amazing ass that you are? No. No and NO! I was already alone in every way in this relationship, so much more than just physically.

Unfortunately, like I said earlier, I struggle with detaching from people. Moreover, narcissists are masters of making one feel unworthy and dependent. Even worse, we were still in contact after the breakup. Yes, to my own detriment, I continued to hold onto the communication between us until one fine day when I learned that he was dating someone in his brokerage. It was a very clarifying moment that I am actually extremely grateful for.

So as I said, in classic form, this man was always saying what he needed to say to be who he wanted to be, not who he really was. There was very little that was authentic, very little care for anyone but himself. After getting over him, it was interesting to watch from afar how his entire real estate team disbanded because of his inability to see beyond himself. His temper and bullheaded nature ultimately caused him to leave the brokerage. Interestingly enough, he eventually married his ex-wife's best friend, exposing one more core characteristic of this man—revenge. He is truly the most vengeful person I have ever encountered.

In the end, my silver lining is that it didn't go on for years (like others have) and I started to see the signs early, acted on them, and with that I was proving to myself that I had learned from my past and was trusting myself once again.

"I will always cherish the original misconception I had of you."

~ Unknown

#211

I met #211 online and after a brief chat, we decided to meet for a drink. When we met, he immediately started talking about the real estate industry.

"I've been in real estate forever. You know that, right?" he asked me. "No I don't know that," I responded, finding the question odd. *Why would I have known this?*

As he said this I was thinking, *I asked him for his last name and did a web search and there was basically nothing on him. If he were in real estate for less than an hour, there would be 5 pages of "stuff." It's the nature of the business.*

He then began to tell me all about himself. He had been divorced for two years, amicable relationship with his wife, two kids, lives in Grosse Pointe, family history in that area, and then made it a point to tell me that he was a member of an exclusive club in Detroit. I knew some members there and as he shared some of what he liked to do, I recognized that we had a friend in common. I mentioned our mutual friend and shared that he and his wife were good friends and past clients of mine. He picked up his phone and called him, right then and there. Then he proceeded to talk to him in a cryptic manner.

Once he hung up, he said, "Yeah, he said you're not worth a damn as a real estate agent."

He would never say that—good friend, good client, and he referred me to his family and to many other colleagues! Lie number one.

All of this was awkward and extremely ego driven. The pontificating was over the top! We then were leaving and walking to our cars. I went for the goodbye hug and he went for the big kiss, with hands traveling to places they were not welcomed to go. He then said he couldn't believe that we were not going to make-out in the car.

He continued to text briefly again, cryptically, and then asked if I wanted to get together on Saturday. We could go to downtown Detroit; I casually said yes and that we'd talk closer to the day. As we got closer, he said Saturday at 9:00 pm worked for him. *9:00 at night?* So I asked him why so late?

"Because this is how it needs to be. It's the time that works for me. I have things to do during the day," he replied.

I contemplated calling it off. So as I was contemplating my "go, no go" decision, I thought, *I'm going to call my friend and ask what they think of this person.* So I did just that, and the response was, "Do you mind if I put you on speaker? We are both here and want to talk about this with you." *Oh boy, ... I knew my hesitant instincts were on point.*

"Have you done a web search on him? I think you should because there is something you need to know that will pop up immediately when you do."

At that moment, it dawned on me that I didn't go back and research who this guy was in real estate. I should have because by the time I left our first date, I knew he must have intentionally misspelled his last name. His family owns a boutique brokerage in a very small community. It would have absolutely popped up in the web search!

"What am I going to see?" I asked.

`"He is the realtor who was having sex with his mistress in the houses he had listed a couple years ago. It was all over the news. Do you remember hearing about that?"

Oh, I remembered hearing about this "person" on the news! What the what? Sure enough, I did a search and there it all was, five pages of every-thing. He was married at the time and was involved with a woman who was also married. This man would list homes and he would use the homes as a place to sleep with his mistress, unbeknownst to the owners or potential buy-ers of the homes. It was a big ordeal in the news, with divorces and lawsuits and lots of scandal.

Immediately, I texted him asking him to call me about our plans, which he did.

When he asked what was up I was perfectly honest and said, "Well, after we met I looked up your brokerage and realized that you misspelled your last name when I asked for it. So today when I did a web search with the cor-rect spelling of your last name, you know what I saw. I have a lot of concerns about meeting with you this evening."

At that point, the true colors of this narcissist were ready to spin. He went on a five-minute, frenetic rant of victimization and denial. I am talking about 100% denial, not just partial "the truth is somewhere in the middle" denial. He said that EVERYTHING stated was a lie. Not one ounce of truth to any of it. His now ex-wife and him are on good terms and of course the woman he was sleeping with was crazy! Yes, he did sleep with her, but that's not why they divorced. The situation was not at all as bad as the media made it out to be.

While he spun this verbal tornado, all I could think was, *Not as bad? This was awful! You were being sued for five million dollars, for Pete's sake. This was terrible. You can't tell me this was not why you got divorced. This is SO why you got divorced! Along with the affair! Along with being sued! Along with being an unethical idiot!*

He adds, "My wife is still part of the brokerage! Everything is good between us!"

She is probably a part of the brokerage because it was a part of the divorce settlement. Who are you kidding?

I waited for him to finish his tirade, mostly because I was in sheer astonishment that someone could be this detached and non-consequential. At the end he rudely blurted out, "So are we going to go out tonight or what?"

"No, we are not."

"I can't *believe* that! I told you the real story!"

"I am not comfortable with any of this." Then, I went on to add, "Your side is SO far out there that there is no way I can trust you. No reason for me to believe anything you say. So there is absolutely no reason for me to go out with you."

He brushed it off and we hung up.

In the days that followed, he sent several friend requests on social media and called and left messages to see if I would like to get together. Was he forgetting the conversation? But isn't that the narcissist! They forget what happens, spin it to their story, think it moves under the rug, and they will be forgiven. It will all be forgotten, and they can now get what they want. The challenge got the best of him on this one. Rejection only breeds more spinning, and in this case I just let him spin. I never answered any of his attempts.

On a total side note of "the ironic," a couple of months after this, I was on first date #216 and we started talking about some of our crazier dates. As I was describing this very experience with #211, he looked at me with anxious eyes and told me that he had actually went on a date with the mistress that #211 was sleeping with in all of the listed homes! He basically finished the story for me and knew all about the situation. We both couldn't stop laughing ... an amazingly small world. ...

"A narcissist mindset.
That didn't happen, and if it did, it wasn't that bad,
and if it was, it's not a big deal, and if it is, I didn't mean to do it,
and if I did, that was your fault."

~ E. S.

#231

This date—non-date really—happened recently and in my own way I feel it was almost karma that brought this man into my life for a fast and furious, here-and-gone timeframe, to almost review all I have learned and then close the door on it all!

#231 was an interesting one. We met online and he was a "lets move to text" quickly kind of guy. Those of you who have been dating online know there are those types. They either message forever or they move to text in a New York minute! This went to texting fast and he saw me on two platforms, so he was "liking" and messaging me on both, almost like he didn't realize it was the same person? Who knows really! So we moved to text and within 24 hours he sent me an absolutely non-solicited "dick pic"… *REALLY? Do I even know your last name?* I personally have no desire for these EVER. I realize some people enjoy this exchange and to each their own. From my perspective, this is not my thing and especially out of my realm of thought within the first 24 hours of texting!

Eventually I chatted with this guy who was "in sales," aka an engineer—*we all know how I feel about that now, don't we?* Then, after we spoke, he wanted to go to a concert. He made this elaborate plan that entailed him coming over NOW so he could have sex with me before we went on the date. *What the hell?* At that point I shared that I wasn't going to have him over or go to a concert with him and we simply were not on the same page of dating.

"Wow! I just put you in my phone. Just wanted to go see a show with you and have fun. I guess not."

I just put you into my phone? I never realized that was a status! Apparently, it was for him.

I texted him back. "Again, I am going to decline on going out because

I just don't think we are in the same lane at this time. We want different things from a relationship. As I said, it's been fun flirting and chatting. Truly, all the best to you, and thank you."

Never say no to a narcissist.

"Wow! That's a total kick in the ass! I do want a long term relationship!"

All I could think was, *How in the hell can you be looking for a long-term relationship? You're leading with sex and you completely take no action on anything that you say. You want to do something but then you never do it. You cowered right out of the last date we tried to plan, and then it was my fault. And all of these point, counter-points that you have are all to totally circumvent what's really happening. This is just one more line of bullshit to serve your story.*

He followed up, "So you really are not going with me to this thing? That is one of the shittiest things anyone could do."

"Total asshole move," he added.

Looking back, I should have cut him off at this point, but I was SO annoyed. I had to respond.

"Really? Honestly, I don't get that long-term vibe from you. It feels heavy on fun and whatever happens happens. I don't see you into me more than sexually. You've asked very few questions about me as a person, and don't come off as very interested or compassionate to my world. Perhaps there is an outer shell to you that I don't know. I am just sharing what I have interpreted. And, by the way, telling me that this is an asshole move doesn't help. It doesn't feel very respectful and I have done nothing to you but share my honest thoughts. Respectfully. ..."

"Really?" he replied. "You are really not even all that hot. Get over yourself. And by the way, you backed out twice. This is why guys treat women like shit. Glad I learned early that you are completely unreliable."

It was now time for silence, so silence it was.
Interestingly, more than a month later, I got two calls from him, of which I didn't answer. Then I get a text.

"Denise?"

I then replied, "Hi. I am not quite sure why you are messaging me. Things did not end very nicely last time we chatted. I don't think we are the right match, friendship or otherwise. I wish you all of the best. Hope things are going well for you.—Denise."

"Just came across your contact and wanted to meet you," he responded.

Again, I responded with silence.

The kicker here is that in less than 2 weeks he illustrated to me that he was everything I should never date. Narcissist. Engineer. Always the victim. Sagittarian. Smoker. Name caller. Drama seeker. Does no wrong. Knows all. Condescending. Ego driven. Lacking compassion and empathy. No thank you.

Everything I should never date ever again!

I told you this chapter was going to be a little heavy! Unfortunately, there are many others that I could share in this category, but remember this book isn't about dwelling on the bad, but instead, moving forward through whatever Good Story comes your way! The beauty of my evolution is that I learned, and oddly enough it had to be through the ridiculousness of these men (and many others) who sadly really exist! I don't believe I can teach anyone to truly see a narcissist. They appear in sheep's clothing. That's the tricky part! The only advice I can give is to hold true to yourself, give everyone a chance, the charismatic ones and even the charmers. … Just watch carefully, follow your instincts, intuition, or gut. Even if you get in deep with one of these narcissistic types, always know there is a way out. Forgive yourself often and start heading in the direction of UP. You'll gain momentum and see it all very clearly in the rear view mirror. It's NEVER too late to step away from a bad relationship. NEVER!

Chapter Nine

THE THINGS WE DO FOR LOVE

#20

Many Good Times (Good Dates).

Have you ever met someone who you had great chemistry with, lots of fun, family values in common, yet dated infrequently over years of time, just hoping one of these years it will be "the right timing?" Well I sure did!

This started off a little oddly. I actually met him through a friend that used to be my boss. She needed a date for my sister's wedding, was currently broken up with her longtime boyfriend, so she asked a CPA she met in her building. They came and we were all introduced. He seemed nice, and at that time I thought nothing of it.

Later in that same year my friend rekindled with her longtime boyfriend and got married. Ironically, the day I was going to go to dinner with her to celebrate and catch up, I ran into the CPA on my way up to her office. While I was sitting in her office the CPA called her. He said his office was remodeled and if we wanted to come down and see the new space, he would love to give us a tour. So we did!

He had a great personality; we all chatted and laughed a bit. He gave me his card, for some odd reason (I was so young and naïve) and my friend and I set off to dinner for celebration and chitchat time!

Throughout the next few days, I kept thinking to myself, *Hmmm, he may have given me his card because he is interested in me; he talked a lot with me and was flirting a bit. Maybe I should call him.*

About a week later, I called and left him a message (again, this was before there was texting). He then called me back and asked if I would like to go with him to see a play at Meadowbrook Hall, which I replied, "I would love to!" The night of the play, I particularly remember the drive to Meadowbrook when he asked how old I was.

"I'm 23," I said. When he heard this, he literally slammed the breaks, acting shocked in his own comical way. He had just turned 30, so he played up his shock, which made me laugh.

As I got to know him, I found him to be one of the most charismatic, fun, kind, and philanthropic people I ever met. He was (and I am sure still is) a good man. So it is no surprise that after about three weeks of casual dating, I was coming to a serious point and wanted to know where we stood in the relationship—a not-so-smart move only a young woman would make. Today, I always say that if you have to ask a man this question, you already know the answer. Nonetheless, my young-self asked.

"Oh, I don't really know. … Just kind of having fun. …" What I thought could be a relationship pretty much ended at that point.

However, what makes #20 a bit of a phenomenon is the pattern that then began. I first went out with him in 1993. Interestingly, I would repeatedly run into him at least once a year, many times in the month of November around his birthday, and then we would have lunch or drinks or go to a concert or dinner … and then I wouldn't see him again for another year or so. This went on from 1993 to 2008; during this span of time I cannot tell you how many times I would think to myself, "Oh my gosh, I think it might work this time!" I actually ran into him once again about a year ago and the interaction was identical. The only difference was there was no follow up date or call. Perhaps the pattern had died when I got married. Perhaps the pattern should have never existed.

He was married and divorced young, and had very few known serious relationships after that over the years. As wonderful as he was, it just didn't seem to be what he was looking for and it was always what I was looking for.

That said, he was ALWAYS a Good Date and we ALWAYS had fun!

Timing is everything. …What an understatement that is!

Work Crush

I was 27 years old when this goofy thing happened! I had a huge crush on a guy that I worked with, but I had no idea how to approach him. Like most 27 year olds, I overthought the whole thing. As a result, I decided that I was going to leave him a voicemail one Friday afternoon, with a compelling call-to-action message—what it was exactly for that weekend I don't remember. However, the plan was he would get the voicemail on Saturday and hopefully call me, and I would see him that weekend. I thought it was a brilliant plan—one way or another, I would know if he was interested in me!

It took me at least 45 minutes to record this message, and it took me several hours before that to formulate in my head what the message would be. The effort I put into this was ridiculous! I would record the message, erase, rerecord, erase, hang up, practice it, call again, record, erase, rerecord … until it was finally perfect! Now I just had to wait for his call.

Saturday came, and there was no response. Sunday came—still no response. All I could think of was that I had to return to the office Monday feeling completely embarrassed. My compelling call-to-action was a bust! Now I felt rejected.

At the time, I was the human resources director for a small builder. As the HR director, I was also the office manager, so I had control over the phone system. I went in on Monday earlier than usual and went into the closet where the big phone system computer was. I knew that if I looked up his extension, I would be able to see if in fact he received and heard the voicemail. So much power, right? So I looked, and the voicemail was never opened. I wasn't sure if I was relieved or sad.

I walked out of the closet and for a moment I actually felt better. At least I wasn't rejected. Then, I got to my desk and felt a rush of regret. *Oh my God! Leaving that message was such a total mistake. I wonder if I can delete it!* Back in the closet I went. I looked up his extension once again and, sure enough, I had the power to delete it … so I did!

The possibility of rejection versus the power of the delete button.
Delete gets the win!

Three Date Monday

With online dating, people can have a first date every day of the week if they are so inclined. With my 236 first dates over a span of 32-plus years, there have been a few days where I had two first dates in one day. Not a lot, but it did happen. However, there was only one time that I had three dates in one day. This spontaneously happened on a random Monday in August of 2019.

On this Monday, I had lunch with a gentleman that I met online who was a professor. He was a very kind man looking for a meaningful relationship. However, he was extremely introverted and, in fact, shared that he was very uncomfortable and avoided going to public places and parties. At the time, I really wished we could have seen each other more, but I knew that the part of him that was extremely introverted would not work for me; I am an outgoing person who enjoys being around energetic and vibrant people. I personally love public events and parties! I need someone with confidence who can "hold their own" in that kind of setting. Unfortunately, this was one of those situations where I wished we were more compatible in that area because he was such a quality person.

The second date of the day was the spontaneous addition to an already planned "two-first-dates" day. He was a man that I had gone out with once or twice months prior and he had resurfaced in the last couple of weeks. It was a beautiful, sunny day, and he was going to take his convertible out for a ride and wanted to know if I would like to catch a drink with him, which sounded great to me because my (now) third date wasn't until 8:00pm, so off I went!

I told him that I had plans at eight, so we decided to go to a particular bar and grill in the area. I showed up around 5:30 and he wasn't there. I thought, *He's probably running late. Maybe traffic is bad*, and found a seat at the bar. I then got a text from him saying, "Are you here?" I texted back that I was, and then called him.

"I am sitting at the bar," I said. "Where are you?"

"I am sitting right outside," he said.

"Oh my gosh, did I pass you?" I asked as I walked outside to see if he was there.

"You are literally standing outside the door?"

"Yep," he said. It suddenly dawned on me.

"Oh, wait a minute. Which one are you at? What are you look-ing at when you are standing outside? Do you see a big soccer field house across the street?" I asked.

"Yep! That's what I am looking at," he responded, and then it dawned on him. "Oh my God. We talked about this—I am at the wrong one! I am so sorry!"

"You know what, don't worry at all. I know exactly where you are. I will drive to that location; it's closer to my next destination any-way, so the 20 minute drive will be that much more time we can spend together later. Go in and get a drink—no worries. I will see you soon!"

When I got there, he was still all wound-up in the fact that he went to the wrong place, but I was able to help him shake it off, and we ended up having a good time catching up. He was a good guy, an attorney, and very down to earth. He explained that the reason he was off the radar for a few months was because he got back together with his old girlfriend for a short while, but that relationship again ended. Like I said, we had a wonderful time talking, and then I had to leave for my "appointment" at eight. He walked me to my car, gave me a big hug and kiss goodbye (a first kiss, at that) and we agreed that we should definitely get together again because we both really enjoyed each other's company.

So I drove off to meet date number three of the day, and I was going to make it there right on time! This was another man that I met online and was meeting for the first time. We were meeting at a restau-rant at an outdoor mall that was a halfway point for both of us. As I was waiting at a crosswalk to let people cross the street before pulling into the parking area, I saw a tall, extremely attractive man walking toward the restaurant. *Wow, that man is super attractive.* As he pulled his phone out to text, I realized that he was my date! *Oh, he is really cute—he really lives up to his pictures!*

I parked and walked into the restaurant, and I was welcomed with a big hug. Before this meeting, we had many good, meaning-ful conversations and texts, and it was so great to finally meet him in person. We sat at a quaint wine bar and talked about many personal things. He was a widower, so we talked about how his wife passed away. We also talked about his children, his work, his childhood and where he grew up. The conversation was a nice ebb and flow between lighter subjects and deeper topics, and the chemistry between us was pretty strong.

In a blink of an eye, it was 10:15 pm and the bar started to flicker the lights to signal that they wanted to close (being that it was a Monday night). We both looked around and realized that we were the only people left, so we closed out the bill and left the restaurant.

As we were walking out, he said, "You know, I don't want this date to end."

"I don't either," I said with a smile.

"I don't know what we can do at this point," he added.

"Well, all the restaurants are probably closing now, but this is an outdoor mall, so we could walk around the mall and continue to talk for a while," I suggested. "It really is a beautiful night."

So we strolled the outdoor walkways while he held my hand. After three laps around the mall, we decided to sit on one of the park-like benches as we continued to talk. We sat on that bench on that beautiful summer night, talking, laughing, and kissing for two and a half hours. It was truly one of the nicest, most wonderful first dates I have ever had. After that night, we texted or spoke every day and went out again about a week later, which was equally as wonderful as this night was.

That last date was a Tuesday. On Wednesday, we texted back and forth throughout the day about each of our workdays. One thing that was charming is that he always ended each of his texts with two kiss emojis—"kiss kiss!"

That Thursday, I texted him for our "good morning" chat, again asking him how he was doing and how his morning was going … and there was no response. Nothing all day. I thought, *That's really strange.*

On that Friday, I knew that he had a heavy court situation to deal with, so I texted him that morning with a supportive message, asking him to give me a call or text to let me know how it all goes. … Again, nothing, and just like that, *Poof!*—he was gone.

I never heard from him again. I also never heard again from the second date of the day. Days after our happy hour date, his aunt (who was very much like a mother to him) passed away, which put him under the radar once again. Then his kids moved back up to college, which filled his schedule, so timing for us was simply off.

I think it is safe to say that my Three Date Monday was quite an anomaly, especially with the perfect third date that went *Poof!* In the end, it was a great Monday, filled with Good Dates! I have no regrets and would do it all over again.

The things we do for love. ... Always trying. Always hoping. ...

Chapter Ten

WAS HE MARRIED? ...YES!

#183

The Bar Rail Musical Chairs

With heavy traffic in a busy business district, I decided to pop into a steakhouse that I frequent often for a drink and to let traffic lighten up before I continued on home. I sat down and was talking with one of the bartenders that I know well. Meanwhile, people started naturally rotating around the bar, coming and going. Sometimes it is like musical chairs! You sit, then someone needs 3 spots so you shift and shift back. I ordered some food and during this time I chatted with a grocery store owner on my left who was with his wife. We talked about the Eastern Market in Detroit. Then there was a man in his eighties on my left who was enjoying a scotch and reading a newspaper ... a real newspaper! The smell of his newspaper—that distinct smell that I haven't experienced in so many years because, let's face it, who reads the newspaper anymore—caught my attention and I immediately started chatting with the man about the flash back moment I just experienced. I was having a lovely conversation with this gentleman, actually with everyone around me. Suddenly, this extremely tall guy (I am talking 6'8") walks into the bar and sits two seats down from me. I find that people that are this tall naturally demand the attention of the room. He was a good-looking guy wearing a nice suit, and I glanced and saw that he was wearing a wedding ring. Meanwhile, the couple I was talking to on my left ended up leaving while I continued to talk to the older gentleman with the newspaper.

New guests entered the bar area and needed a shift in seats, so the tall guy came over and sat right next to me.

"I hope that's okay," he said as he sat down in the seat.

"Sure, that's no problem at all. I am just finishing my drink," I responded.

"You seem super friendly. I've been watching you talk with the people around you and the older gentleman next to you," he added. Meanwhile, the older gentleman cashed out and left the bar.

"Yes, he was reading a newspaper! It really brought me back!"

We began to have a nice conversation. Don't get me wrong; I remembered that I saw a wedding ring on his finger. I immediately noticed when he sat next to me that he *didn't* have his ring on.

We were making small talk and then he started asking me all about my love life. "You are an attractive woman, friendly, outgoing—I can't believe you are not dating anyone."

I decided to turn the conversation onto him. He talked about how he had a son, along with how he was an attorney for a locally well-known, ambulance-chasing law firm, which I thought made the situation even more hilarious. He never mentioned anything about a wife, and he quickly pivoted and started asking me questions again.

"No no no, let's get back to you," I responded. "So what happened to your son's mom?" He started nervously laughing and changed the subject once again, and the conversation continued, until he had to go to the restroom. When he did, the bartender came up to me.

"Denise, you know he's married, right?"

"Yep! I saw the ring,"

"Okay. ... Did you say anything to him?"

"Not yet, but I will," I said with a smirk.

"Okay, I just didn't want you getting into something you didn't realize."

I totally appreciated her caution for me; she knew that I was single and she was watching this married man come on to me like a freight train. As she walked away, he came back, and it was time. ... I couldn't help myself.

"Okay, so are we going to talk about your wife or are we not going to talk about your wife ... at all?"

Shocked, he answered, "Well, what do you mean?"

"When you were sitting two seats down, you had a ring on, but by the time you moved to sit next to me, the ring was off. I don't really want to know where the ring went, but I know it was on, and now it's off ... and that's all I really need to know."

He just stared at me as I continued.

"So you are married? Are we going to talk about this person who you are married to, that I assume is the mother of your child? OR, are you going to ignore that this is even a possibility?"

"Wow, you are really outspoken."

"I'm not outspoken. You had the damn ring on."

"You looked?" he asked.

"Yes, I did—you're six foot eight, for God's sake! Everybody saw you when you walked into this room. ... Yeah, I looked at your hand to see if you were married—absolutely. However, I saw that you were married and I respect the ring, a little more than you do, apparently."

He just laughed and smiled while I spoke, and then said, "Well, all right then. You just call it like you see it!"

"Yes I do," I said as we kept talking. He then talked about his relationship with his wife. Of course, it was a "loveless marriage"—they always are—and then he asked me, "Do you think we could get together at some point?"

"We could possibly get together for lunch. There might be things that cross in our paths that could help each other professionally," I responded, especially after talking at length about the fact that he just bought a new home.

We finished our drinks and then both of us went to get our cars from valet. When I went to give him a hug goodnight, he responded, "That's all I get?"

"Yes, absolutely, because you are married. Put the ring back on. You're going home." He had a laughing smirk now, as if to say, *Oh my God, I can't even believe you! This is hilarious!*

We had exchanged cards, and of course he called me after we met. The conversation went to him devising a plan for a lavish affair.

"We could travel together. I have a client in Chicago. You could come with me and we could spend the weekends together. That would be wonderful."

I thought, *No, we can't do something like that. I don't care if he is in a loveless marriage*. This is ridiculous. Since when did I become a prostitute? Needless to say, that never happened. What is funny is that to this day, we have remained Facebook "friends" (I don't know when that happened—probably right after we met) and he is consistently one of the first ten people to 'like' anything I post. I have had the chance to watch his son grow up, see pictures of he and his wife who are still married, and watch what appears to be a very good life.

Do I see him as a terrible human being? No, I don't. I think he is incredibly unhappy, and I am absolutely sure he is having affair after affair, instead of making the changes he needs to make himself happy … or maybe his marriage isn't as loveless as he said it was. … I'll never know!

"A man on a date wonders if he'll get lucky. The woman already knows."

~ Monica Piper

#218
Lots of Energy

I met this man on an online dating site. We had some nice conversations on the phone after connecting online. He lived close by, which I thought was great. We quickly decided to get together and meet for coffee one afternoon. As usual, I got his last name prior to meeting so that I could do a quick search on him. Everything seemed pretty normal; it appeared that he owned his own accounting practice. So far, all good.

I arrived first and bought a bottle of water, and then he arrived shortly after … in a jogging outfit. Even funnier, everywhere he went, as he grabbed his coffee from the barista or realized he forgot a cup warmer, he was literally jogging. Immediately I was cracking up. In his online profile he answered the question, "What would your third grade teacher say about you?" His response was, "Lots of energy." As he was jogging everywhere, all I could think of was, *His third grade teacher was right on. … Lots of energy! So hilarious!*

So we sat and talked, and he seemed like a very nice guy. He did have lots of energy, with a sort of nervous energy in his conversation. He talked about his family and kids, and he also talked about his brother, who was in real estate and sounded very familiar to me, along with lots of odds and ends. I couldn't seem to connect the dots on a lot of levels, and I was starting to sense a bit of disconnect with what he was talking about, which made me even more curious.

Because of this, after we met, I went online to check and see if he was actually divorced. He said he was divorced, and yet he didn't seem to have any custody schedule with his kids and never spoke of the times they would be with him or his ex-wife—all the normal things you hear from a parent that is actually divorced. There didn't even seem to be a separate residence involved. Lots of red flags were popping up!

It occurred to me that divorce records are public records, so I decided to see if there was anything I could dig up online that would show some proof that he was truly divorced. The records showed that he filed four weeks prior to us meeting, and they also showed that they had also filed two other times. They filed back in 2011, and then didn't get a divorce. They filed in 2015…again, no divorce. The odds of this couple following through didn't look good. I know that people say "third times a charm" but I don't. I remember him mentioning that the divorce was "super amicable." … Sure it was. It didn't even start yet!

He did contact me after our first meeting, and I did find out that his brother was in fact the man I knew for years in real estate. I also was completely honest with him, sharing that I knew that he just filed and that this was the third time around. I simply let him know that he needed to walk down that path completely before I put myself in a position where I would be involved with someone who may or may not get divorced.

In the big picture, I do not knowingly date anybody who hasn't been divorced for at least a year!

If a man doesn't connect the dots for me, I will gladly do it for him.
In this case, was he married? … Legally he was!

White Escalade Guy

I need to explain the back-story to this Good Story. ...

My brother-in-law would always tell me that I didn't pay attention to people around me who were watching me, which honestly is very accurate. He said he could be driving next to me, waving like a lunatic and honking his horn, and I still would be all "ten-and-two" hands on the steering wheel, eyes straight ahead.

That said, one day I was driving down 16 Mile Road in my little white Avenger, and there was a white vehicle that was completely in sync with what I was doing—whether I drove fast or slowly, he was right there—and I thought to myself, This is so weird! I took a good look to my left, and the vehicle that was following my every move had now shifted lanes. There again was this big, white Escalade. *Well isn't this goofy!*

So I kept driving and he then moved to my right side and stayed in sync. I looked over at the driver and he waved at me, so I waved back. He then motioned for me to roll my window down, so I did just that. *My brother-in-law would be so proud of me!* I thought.

"Hey, hi! You are really attractive!" he said as we drove side by side.

"Thank you!"

"Can you pull over?" he asks.

"Okay. ..." *What am I thinking? Safety first, right? Apparently not!*

So I pulled over in a TGI Friday's parking lot; it's a well-populated area. I thought, *Safety first is now kicking in!* I parked but I didn't get out of my car. I decided to role down my passenger window while he parked next to me and got out of the Escalade. He came to the open window and handed me his business card, saying, "It is really great to meet you. You are a very pretty woman. We should go to lunch sometime."

I laughed and said, "This is so funny! ... Yeah, sure. Why not?" I looked down at his card and he worked for some kind of construction company, and I sold new home construction at the time. I then took a good look at him as he spoke. Nice looking guy. Gorgeous watch—at the time I was totally into watches. *Hmmm. ... This could be good!*

He took my card, got back in his Escalade, and drove away. Later that evening, around 10:30pm, I got a blocked call. The caller left no message. About two hours later, about 12:30am, I got another blocked call. No message.

The next day, a third blocked call came up at about 2:30pm in the afternoon. I was working from home and decided to pick up the phone to see who this was. It was White Escalade Guy! He said he wanted to call and get to know me. He asked me the regular questions anyone asks when first meeting someone—have you ever been married, do you have any kids, the usual "stuff."

"What about yourself?" I ask him.

"Well, I work in the building industry, I am married, and I—"

"What?" I totally interrupted him. "I'm sorry. What did you just say?"

"Well, I'm married. I want to be honest and all."

"Okay. ..."

"I mean, is that going to cause a problem?"

"Uh, yes, that's going to cause a very big problem," I answered.

"Well, I mean, I am being very forthright about it," he said.

"Yeah," I said. "I don't really care if you are being forthright about this. I care more about not being a home wrecker."

"A lot of people really don't have a problem with this."

"I am not 'a lot of people' and I have a BIG problem with this," I said.

"Well, why do you have a big problem with this? What if you weren't really happy in your marriage and you just wanted to meet other people?" he asked.

"Okay, this is getting SO much worse than it was in the beginning when you were just telling me that you are married. At the end of the day, you are looking for a hook-up and I am NOT going to sleep with someone else's husband *knowingly* because I would never want someone to sleep with my husband *knowingly.* So I will thank you for being honest. However, I DO NOT want to have lunch with you."

"Are you sure?" *Am I sure? Of course I am sure!*

"Yes, I am absolutely sure. Again, thank you for being honest, but we are pretty much done here," and with that, we hung up.

Later that evening, around 11:30pm, he called once again, and he continued to call every night for three nights, assuming it was him. I never answered.

Wow! I couldn't wrap my head around that on any moral level whatsoever. Yet he was completely fine with it. I am sure many women are, as well, but I am just not that gal.

The funniest part of this whole story is that I called my brother-in-law right after meeting White Escalade Guy that sunny afternoon.

"You are never going to believe this. I met this guy while driving!" I said, giggling. "Seems like a nice looking guy. Let's see what happens!"

Twenty-four hours later, I called my brother-in-law back, again.

"Yep, I think I am just fine with my blinders on, hands at 'ten-and-two,' listening to music, alone, because look what happens when I meet people on the road!"

OH, how we laughed!

Married guy, cruising the boulevard for chics on a sunny weekday afternoon. ... Didn't see that coming!

Chapter Eleven

ONE OF THE GOOD ONES:

#120
The Closest Thing to Perfect

In April of 2008, I was working as a sales rep for a benefits administration company. I was unexpectedly told that I had to attend an expo at the Townsend in Birmingham. It was something completely thrown into my schedule last minute. As I was driving to the event, my boss called me and told me that I had to speak to one person in particular who wasn't at the last event. She went on and on about why, along with something about him jumping off a cliff in Hawaii and breaking something. … To be honest, I was barely listening because I felt dragged into something I had no interest in doing, nor did I understand how this was benefitting my book of business.

Once I got there, I set up my little booth and then stood and networked. Suddenly, this tall, sparkly blue-eyed, good-looking man came up to my booth to say hello. He said he knew my boss, Kay, and he was happy that our company was able to join in the expo. I remember distinctly that his blue eyes lit up when he spoke. However, I was still in my disengaged mode, so at the moment his charm was lost on me. All I could think of was, *I really don't want to be here.*

Later that morning, there was going to be a presentation by the expo sponsor. I was standing at a tall cocktail table in a conference space, eating a quick breakfast before it began. Suddenly, the man who approached me earlier came back to talk to me.

"So Kay told me that you were going to be pinch-hitting for her today," he said with a smile.

It suddenly dawned on me.

"Oh, you are the guy who jumped off the cliff!" I said excitedly, now that the dots were connecting in my head.

"What?" he said with a surprised smirk.

"Yes, you were in Hawaii and you jumped off a cliff. I heard the whole story this morning!" I said. "I don't exactly know why I heard this story, but why were you jumping off of a cliff? What in the world were you doing?"

He immediately started laughing. "Oh my gosh, I can't believe you know all of this."

"I can't either," I said, cracking up, "but I heard the whole thing this morning. What were you doing? Cliff diving?"

He explained that he was in Hawaii with his family and yes, he was cliff diving and landed on his back, which put him in traction for a full month. He then asked if I was going in to see the presentation.

"Oh yes, I should go get a seat," I said while realizing it was about to begin. He went his way and I went mine.

The presentation started and who was introduced as the CEO of the organization putting the expo on? Of course, ... the man who jumped off the cliff! He came out and spoke to the audience about why his California-based brokerage was expanding to Michigan, and so forth. As he spoke, I thought to myself, *Oh my gosh, who would have known he was all this.... He is beyond charming, cute as can be, and surprisingly very real. I like this!*

So the presentation ended, and he came back over to talk to me as I was packing up the booth. He asked if he would see me at the next presentation in Grand Rapids on that Thursday.

"Yes, I will be there," I said.

"See you then," he said, with his kind, lit-up eyes, and off we went.

The morning of the Grand Rapids presentation came, and he came up to me before the presentation and gave me a big hug. He seemed very excited to see me, but I thought, *He's probably like this with everyone because this is just who he is—a kind man with lots of charisma. It's probably just how he treats everyone.*

I was with two other people from my company at this particular expo. We did our expo display and then watched the presentation once again. After, I had lunch with my boss and co-workers at the restaurant in the hotel. He and his team were also having lunch at the same restaurant before heading back to California. When I asked for our bill, the server told me that our bill was handled.

"Handled? What do mean it was handled?" I asked, completely confused.

"Your bill was handled by someone else," the server said.

When we were leaving, I approached his table with his team talking amongst one another. I quietly made eye contact with him and said, "Thank you." He looked down a moment in a bashful way, and then looked back up at me. Hilariously, everyone else at this huge table looked right at me as well, all at the same time, as if to say, "Who are you?" and "Who bought what lunch?"

I smiled and said, "That was very generous and kind of you. Again, thank you," and then I left.

Very interested in this charming man, I sent him a thank you card with my card in it, and shortly after I got a voicemail from him saying that it was wonderful meeting me and that he hoped to see me again sometime soon. At this point, I was in the process of changing companies. I reached out to him before I took the new job to get his thoughts about the new company. The phone call led to a very fun conversation, which led to many fun conversations. This lead to our first date on August 14, four months after we first met. He was coming into town and asked me to have dinner with him. We went to a trendy Asian restaurant in the area, and then went to the Townsend's bar where he was staying to have another cocktail there. I remember it being such a wonderful, laid-back evening as we talked, laughed, and watched the summer Olympics on the big screens above. The night ended with him walking me to my car and giving me a very memorable kiss good night before leaving.

The next morning, he called me first thing on his way to the airport, excited to see me again and hoping we could work something out very soon. From that point on, we talked on the phone every day and soon it was going to be Labor Day weekend.

"I don't have anything going on this weekend for Labor Day," he said to me. "What have you got going on?"

"Nothing really," I said.

"Would you want to come to California?"

That would be amazing!

"Or, if you aren't uncomfortable staying at my house, we could meet in Chicago. Whatever works for you. ..."

"I have never been to California," I said to him. "However, that's your house and your space. If you aren't completely comfortable—"

"No, actually coming to my house would be easier. I am totally comfortable with it if you are," he said.

"Okay, deal!"

So our second date was a first class ticket to California! He sent me the ticket and the itinerary; he took care of scheduling everything. I flew in on Friday and was staying until Monday. Over the course of the weekend, we went to Santa Monica, La Jolla, Belle Aire, Santa Barbara, and more. We also spent time at his gorgeous home, watching documentaries, cooking breakfast, and baking cookies. It was an easygoing weekend with so much charm, romance, and exploration—truly an amazing experience.

Before I flew back on Monday, we talked about him coming to Michigan at the end of September. Unfortunately, by the middle of September, he started distancing himself. By the time it was his 50th birthday in early October, communication was minimal. It took all I had not to reach out to him on his birthday, but I needed to send him a silent message that I knew something was up. The day after his birthday, I got an email from him saying that he felt badly about how he handled several things, and that he was back with a girlfriend that he previously dated for two years. He explained that he was thinking a lot about her after our weekend and that he needed to give it another try. The distance and age difference between us was also an issue.

Heartbroken is an understatement on this one. I cried the entire day after reading this message. I did write him back, thanking him for being honest with me, and for the wonderful person I saw him to be. I did sense something was off and hoped I was wrong, but better to know than to assume or tell myself some crazy story to make me feel bad or turn him into the villain. No one was a villain here. Timing, age difference, and a huge amount of miles between us stacked the deck against what I thought were great odds of happiness. A girl can and should dream!

Our paths did cross a few times and he was always a class act of kindness and charm. In hindsight, there were legitimate obstacles to our relationship. I was the youngest person he had ever dated and, at 38 years old (12 years younger than him), I still felt that children were possible in my future. However, his kids were already grown and in college; he was at a completely different stage in his life, which I am sure contributed to his decision … and of course the distance between Michigan and California isn't a hop, skip, and a jump!

The irony of the distance obstacle is that I wound up going back to work for the original benefit administration company, and with that return my new territory became the state of California. So, early in 2009 I started traveling to California every other week for about a year and a half. It took a while for my mind to stop questioning, "Would I see him on this trip" or "Maybe it could have worked out," but eventually my heart caught up with my head.

He did end up marrying the woman he went back to and I actually had the chance to briefly meet her at a national conference where he was being honored. Even though I was engaged at the time, seeing him, now years later, still made my heart excitedly skip a beat, with a hint of jealousy. Some people will simply always have that effect on you—and he is definitely that person for me.

"To Love & Win is the Best Thing.
To Love & Lose is the next Best Thing."

~ Fortune Cookie

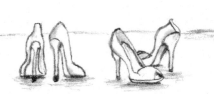

Chapter Twelve

SPEED ROUND: A.D.
(AFTER DIVORCE)

#150 First date after my divorce. My mom was concerned so she asked that I send her a text with how it went when I got home. After the date, I shared he was not really paying attention to me, more so watching the room, and a little self absorbed. ... As soon as I hit "send" I realized it went to my date instead of my mom! Maybe I wasn't ready to date yet!

#152 Claimed he was 55. I'm gonna call BS! He had more work done on his face than I would ever aspire to have done, and he was super particular—he had us meet at his work and gave me a tour of his business. Was this an interview or date? A-Z odd!

#161 Blind date, and not a good match! Then two years later I realized this guy had been seriously dating my client's sister for YEARS! Ironically a dinner with my client's whole family was scheduled and when he came in he was sure shocked to see me. He ignored me and didn't acknowledge that we had ever met. Then, later that evening when we went to my client's house, he was everywhere I was. Next day he decided it was meant to be—US! "I cannot stop thinking of you, and us seeing each other—feels like it's meant to be," he wrote the next day, and continued to say that he and his girlfriend of YEARS decided to take a break last night! OH HELL NO! This was a hard "no" two years ago. ... NO, NO, & NO!

#179 First problem—cheap! And if you were going to try to illustrate chivalry by putting me in the car, you have to shut the door! He opened the car door and then bolted to his driver's side door. What is that? The Half Chivalry Move?

#186 When someone shows you who they are, LISTEN! If only I listened to that advice!

#190 Dr. Rude. Met on a fix-up, double date with my friends. He was their foot doctor. He flew into the restaurant late and immediately announced he needed to leave in 45 minutes to meet his daughter. Really? You should have just rescheduled for the fourth time, or just politely shared with your clients and my friends that you were not interested. So rude and arrogant, and he sure wasn't all that!

#192 & 205 Why did they have to be smokers?

#201 FYI: Don't ask me out to have a drink with you and your friends to celebrate your birthday and then expect me to sleep with you! And when that rude awakening is realized you do not get to pout! After all, you are older now so you should act like a grown-ass man!

#202 The most unavailable guy I had ever met!

#207 One of the best compliments ever .... "No one has ever kissed me like you did yesterday."

#215 The guy who leads with how rich he is along with how he has strong sexual needs, and then spends the entire date bitching how all women are gold-digging tramps. What you put out there always comes right back to you!

#227 When I ask you if your parents still live in the Rochester area, what kind of answer is, "Ahh, maybe, sorta." Was a "yes" or "no" not available or hard to find? I wasn't going to visit them! End game, I don't like vague!

"Single |sin-gle| (adjective) – Too fabulous to settle."

~ Mandy Hale,
The Single Woman: Life, Love, and a Dash of Sass

Reflection

FACING FORWARD

Looking back, no matter if an experience was good or not-so-good, I always dated with intention. I wasn't opening myself up to new people, new experiences, to merely fill the time, nor was I ever looking for a hook-up—I'm sure you know that by now. … never been my style! In fact, I never slept with someone on the first date or had a one-night stand (truth!). From my very first date at 18 until right this moment, I have regarded every first date as a possibility—a possibility of finding true love, or THE ONE (however you phrase that)!

That said, sometimes I look at all of this collectively and think to myself, *How did I have so many Good Stories?* The common thread of these stories is that they are obvious, yet unbelievable. Obvious as in these types of experiences happen to many of us who are single and dating. Unbelievable as in how I ended up with so many Good Stories, yet continued on, and on … and am still continuing on!

If I had to narrow down one reason why I think I had such a variety of experiences, I would say it is the fact that I have always been very open and accepting of new opportunities as they presented themselves. As you read, that doesn't mean I was open and accepting to continue dating every person I met. We know that many of these were "one and done" kind of dates. Some of these "one and done" decisions were my choice and others not on my terms at all. … If only I had that much control all the time, right?

However, without these first dates, who would I be today? They taught me lessons on how the world works, and showed me a variety of personalities that I would never have known if not for that "one experience together." You can sometimes hear in my stories how naïve I was. I didn't even know how to flirt until I was around 30 years old! Even then, I didn't execute with tremendous swagger. Although, what I did execute tremendously was the ability to get back up and try again.

I have always truly believed, "I didn't come this far to only come this far," so I continue to continue on!

Then there are the Good Ones. At the time, I wholeheartedly wished each one of them would have worked out. Yet they all worked out as they were meant to work out. My first was like a hurdle I had to cross to get to what was really important in life—yet I wished he could have lasted forever. My White Horse restored faith with his honesty and showed me a much better example of what love can be. It took a long time to get over him, but I made it through! My California romance— so worth a shot, and so devastated when I was the only one looking to take that shot! My Ex-husband, ... well, you know there is more to that story. Even though the experience taught me that it is NEVER too late to get out of a bad relationship, that heartbreak hurt on levels I didn't know I had.

As for the many other first dates, I would have loved to have had the chance to explore further with many of them. The issues were not always something to be categorized or in my control. Many times, the reasons were logistics, mindset, unknown/unforeseen personal preferences, and good old timing.

Timing ... such a factor! This is true more so in the later years than in my 20's or 30's. I suppose that is where hope, faith, and trust in the process has to come forward within ourselves to keep up the stamina to keep going. Time does what time is supposed to do. Time alone will always help heal a heart. And as I have found, my timing might not be right now, but to learn, grow, and stay open to the enjoyment of the journey is key—and keeping the faith in the belief that love is ALWAYS on time is essential!

Surprisingly, there are very few dates I regret. There are a few I should have cut-off earlier, trusted my instincts, or listened to my inner voice, but all in all, these mistakes were part of the journey. The mistakes taught life and human behavior lessons, the heartbreaks taught resilience, and the journey taught me patience. Through it all, my frequent moments of self-forgiveness and laughter kept my faith, and kept me hopeful—and let's face it, sometimes you have to go far enough to know you went far enough!

Unfortunately these situations can often bring grudges, bitterness, baggage … or whatever you want to call it. The thing is, if you hold on to any of these factors of disappointment, it is also holding on to you, which is ultimately holding you back! That affects YOUR timing! There is very little space for this negativity in the journey. If we give the negativity too much space, it will take us down.

The moral of the story here is that these dates, good or not-so-good, didn't take me to a negative place of bitter, "poor me," or victim—they didn't take me down. Instead, I have kept a sense of humor, happiness, positivity, hope, and a "never give up on your heart's desire" mindset.

What good does it do to be bitter? Conversely, what good does it do to be happy? Really think of those two questions for a minute. Bitter follows you like a nasty cloud. It eats away at you. People can sense it, see it, and most often don't want to spend time with it! Oddly enough, I find that even people who are bitter themselves still reject or step away from others they find bitter. Kind of surprising, right? Not really!

On the other hand, happy attracts happy, feels good, feels light, feels freeing, is just as contagious as bitter, but so much more delightful. So why do people choose bitter? You know what I think? I think bitter allows for giving up. In the vulnerable space needed to be in truly good and healthy relationships, giving up is way easier than leaning in and opening your heart to the possibilities. Even though the possibility of being happy is equally present, most people forget that part and are driven to react from fear and lack. And let's face it, fear and lack are good buddies with bitter—you can see where this is going.

I also find the general public is totally up for giving up—it's a total shame! There is a quote that says something like, "You can have excuses or results, but you can't have both." I couldn't love that message more! You have control in your choices … so why not choose happy?

Thankfully, I have always felt in control of myself within these experiences, even when I was at my weakest or lowest points. I certainly have been discouraged, hurt, and exhausted at times, but the trust and control in myself allowed me to go through these dating experiences and not allow them to define me or my spirit.

One thing this book was never about is a fairy tale ending. It was always meant to be about the journey and my mindset through-out the journey. As you have just walked through the highlights of my dating journal, I am not leaving you with a fairy tale ending … mostly because there isn't one, at least not at this time. You have seen my evolution. You have learned my peeves, my deal breakers, my goofy, sarcastic sense of humor, my tendency for quick judgments, and you have also seen my tenacity, spirit, some grit, and determination.

At the end of the day, with all of these factors, good and maybe not so good—I keep going! I continue to seek my Mr. Right, knowing he is out there, knowing I am worth this relationship I seek, knowing this relationship is still in my future. I often metaphorically say, "My best dance is yet to come." Ultimately, I believe if he is not my Mr. Right, it is never too late to keep trying. If he is my Mr. Right, he is right on time! Ultimately, I am seeking a connection that is real, mutual, respectful, loving, exciting, growing daily, and built to last a lifetime. Truthfully, who isn't? The adjectives will be different for you, as they should be, but your desires, needs, timing, and wants should be held as priority. Settling is not necessary. As speaker, author, and behavioral scientist Steve Maraboli has stated:

> Don't settle … Wait for the one who treats you like an invest
> ment, not a test drive. Someone who inspires you to be your
> best … one who looks beyond your outer beauty and falls in
> love with our soul.

Life is unpredictable and at the same time filled with possibili-ties. With that, I challenge each and every one of you to truly choose happy, … happy to meet new people, happy to have loved and lost, happy to experience great love, happy to be alive, happy to have tried, happy to have failed, and happy to have the strength to continue try-ing! Look at this as a journey, not a destination, and have enormous faith in the middle. So, until that "right on time" relationship, see the value in each experience, keep laughing, trust in yourself, and always remember that it is never too late to start again, if needed. You are SO worth it!

*"Never go in search of love. Go in search of life,
and life will find you the love you seek."*

~ Atticus

ABOUT THE AUTHOR

Denise Lizette, a self-proclaimed expert so-ciologist, can be found working her suc-cessful real estate business by day and ob-serving, even marveling at, human behavior (dating or otherwise normal daily life) every other minute of her waking day. Born and raised in the suburbs of southeast Michigan, this debut book has been on her bucket list for decades. Denise loves to laugh and be-lieves laughter is one of life's best riches!

ABOUT THE ILLUSTRATOR

Jamie Ruthenberg is a Detroit-born author, artist, and illustrator. Currently, she is both the author and illustrator of the Miles Ed-ucational Series, a heartwarming children's book series. As a self-taught artist, Jamie creates her illustrations with a pencil and watercolor paint. Since her launch into the world of illustration in 2015, her detailed artwork has filled the pages of over 12 books, many of which are discussed on her YouTube series, Jamie's Book and a Bite, as well as on her new book reading series

ACKNOWLEDGMENTS

An enormous thank you to all of my family, friends, and forever life supporters!

Thank you, Joan Bellore. Mom, you have always shown me grace, wisdom, and selflessly encouraged my best self to emerge with confidence. I simply wouldn't be who I am today without you as my best friend and world's best mother. I forever love and appreciate you!

Thank you, Michele Avis. Sis, you have been an idol of mine since my first breath. Thank you for your compassionate encouragement, fun time sister-fun, sage advice, and heartfelt connection. … We are unique and irreplaceable! Blessed to be your sister!

Thank you, Cameron and Kendall, my nephew & niece. You fill me with love in so many ways! Grateful to be your Nene!

Thank you to the great men of my life who have continuously and consistently illustrated the values, actions, and traits of exactly that—great men. You instilled faith in me that there is a great man out there for me!

Thank you, Dad, Ray Bellore.
Thank you, Colin Avis.
Thank you, Larry Bellore.
Thank you, Rudy Pilot.
Thank you, Johnny Mazzola.

Thank you, Claudine Kuelske. Who would have thought the day you kindly and humorously bequeathed that refrigerator magnet to one of your only single girlfriends, that it would grace the cover of my first book!

Thank you, Sue Howell (Suzy Q), my favorite friend who just gets me! Your encouragement and giggles every time I shared a new story over the years not only encouraged me to write this but also helped me continue on! Friends like you are once in a lifetime!

Thank you to my Life Coach, Avianna Castro. The peace, patience, and trust you have opened me up to in the past two years is as AMAZING as you are!

Thank you, Jamie Ruthenberg, my illustrator, book collaborator, and friend. Your lovely mother put this connection together years ago (thank you, Marietta)! You have been so beautiful to work with. Your creativity, craft, skills, artistry, and spirit have been steadfast throughout this process. ... Grateful and Blessed!

Thank you all 236 of my first dates who have, unbeknownst to themselves, helped me become the best version of me!

And last but not least, thank you, Darryl English, my first date #237, who has redefined the phrase "the closest thing to perfect." You arrived right on time and are truly above and beyond my expectations of my great man!

START YOUR JOURNEY. ...
START YOUR OWN JOURNAL

YOUR JOURNAL

YOUR JOURNAL

YOUR JOURNAL

YOUR JOURNAL

YOUR JOURNAL

YOUR JOURNAL

YOUR JOURNAL

Made in the USA
Monee, IL
04 April 2021